I'm Gay, And I Hate Myself: American Loser

By

Mark David King

Printed in the United States of America

1.) Poetry

2.) Political Science

3.) Theological Prose

Purchase all of Mark David King's books on Amazon.Com National and International; plus, all Internet bookstores; specifically, here are the titles:

1.) Transcending Twilight: Angels Eclipse Vampires

2.) Is Glenn Beck The Devil? Muhammad Rising . . .

3.) Sean Hannity's Theocracy; Plus, Virgin Mary LIVES!

4.) About Britney Spears And Male Genitalia—An Anthropological Treatise

5.) Khloe Kardashian Meets The Easter Bunny: An American Play

6.) Barack Obama, Do Cyborgs Dream Of Robotic Sheep? An American Poem

7.) Werewolf Slut

8.) A Southern Gothic Werewolf In Nashville

Man being reasonable must therefore get drunk, for what is the best of life but intoxication.

         . . . Lord Byron . . .

Patrick Henry boasted:

"Give me liberty or give me death."

He didn't want 50% of the liberty;

Moreover,

He didn't want 80% of the liberty;

Specifically,

He wanted ALL the liberty!!!

* * * * * *

We have the right to be gay in this country, and we have the right to detest it as well. But put a straight, good-looking man in a maximum security prison in America; next, he will hate the rage of gayness, deploring the demonic dance of sodomy aimed at his masculinity. Verily Mr. President, clean up our prison system, and while those there should receive punishment, they have the ethical right to do their "time" without the interruption of rape.

FOREWARD:

The sublimity of LOVE needs not "tough" to be attached; moreover, if a man does Crystal Meth every morning; then goes and works a 9 hour day 5 days a week, ultimately giving half of that narcotic-induced income to charity; next—is he a bad man? Christ—who gives a shit. Anyway, I have been a naughty, little, sailor man; indeed, I have talked to homosexual men on the Internet, surfed into homoerotic sites, and for a full 10 seconds in my 39 years of life—I actually touched a man inappropriately. After that, he tried to touch me, and I keenly knocked his desirous paw back to its humble side. As a result of that non-sodomized, but highly gay action, I took a hammer and smashed my hand numerous times till freakishly flying on the gusty gallop of 4 wheels to the Emergency room where they put my hand in a spectacular splint and magnanimously prescribed the altruism of pain killers—and I liked it. Being high was not a problem. Was Carl Sagan a malevolent villain for mathematically morphing physics into language readable for the normal Joe after marijuana use? Was Kerouac a cheat for using the pulsating-dance of amphetamines to forge the fantastic of literature? Should those pieces of drug-induced labor be thieved away and locked secret in a macabre abyss? Then why do we scandalize athletes for steroids? Was Captain America not a hero? Were pilots who took "speed" during World War 2 not heroes? Go screw yourself, and while you're at it—

bring me back a joint, cause I don't reside in the regal liberty of the God-

Kissed Country called California. And check me: I'm a bravado-beefed

BAD GUY; I've had gay thoughts. But oh yeah—America is over that now.

Gay is ubiquitous, deserving never the topic of negativity to touch its anal

region, where fecal matter and numerous amounts of uncouth bacteria reside

in wait for thunderous action. But big-mouthed Joy Behar says to Joel

Osteen: "What if gays are born that way?" That being her generous defense

for an asymmetrical part of America's population. Anyway, my question

would be: "What if a pedophile is born that way?" Come on—nobody is

buying my shit—so don't get pissed then Bucko. But straying away from

gay to appease your parental units instead of yourself is a noble thing;

however, most people don't give a damn about the respectful wishes of their

anthropological creators, wanting only to entertain the lascivious lusts that

horrendously haunt their corporeal machines until loss of anal virginity or

the pseudo-experience of intercourse from a plastic penis crafted in a

malicious manufacturing plant, and Bill Clinton likes this I tell ya . . .

Okay—this is America. Motherf%&*$%# best country standing—no

doubt!!! And thank God gays aren't spit on or beat down. I totally gel with

the synergy of them having the bold blessing of marriage as well; still, come on—I don't wanna be a fag at the end of the day. Look, I'll wash their feet, give to H.I.V. charity, even watch Prime Time Television that showcases them on a perpetual cycle of circus-like humor, but Bubba—I don't wanna be one. Yeah, deep down maybe I'm gay. I'm the butt pirate at the end of the day. And that's my perplexing point—I don't wanna . . . Instead, I want to grab some tits; specifically: I WANT SOME VAGINA!!! Hence, I should go get some. Thus, my point is that people should not be conned into embracing ALL of their fantasies. Sometimes we should pedagogue RESISTANCE. Sometimes a bi-sexual is nothing more than a greedy son of a bitch. But God love 'em. Still, while morals should not be the constructor of American laws; nevertheless, they should help spawn the benevolence of the unearthly, human conscience. Too, everybody needs to lay off of Chaz Bono—dude has more stones than most of us. That is all I'm say'n . . .

Dramatis Personae; moreover, cast of players and haters:

SARAH PALIN: The school teacher or Librarian with glasses who sparks the arousal of fantasies with MILFness; specifically, a conservative angel ornamented in Reagan idealism, blessed with buxom abundance, and a true kitten in heat. David Lettermen obviously had a crush on her curvaceous, corporeal aspects since he poked unfit humor into her celebrity stature; plus, she was the former Governor of Alaska, is married to a masculine essence, and has spawned a number of candid children—to the bone. She likes guns and family values, but her attractive face is all the rage that oozes out a sexual charisma to Evangelical Christians, Republicans, and younger men dreaming of entertaining her in the purity of their SpongeBob pajamas. Democrats hate her, for they know she can kick ass in elections. Too, she usurps Nancy Pelosi and Hillary Clinton with having won the Genetic Lottery and being "doable"; thus, the Democrats fear for their lives concerning her flight into futurity.

OPRAH WINFREY: Tells you what to read, implies who to vote for, and wants her pseudo-wisdom to control the world whether being cerebral rape or a perpetuity of shallow vociferousness. A fruity, Existential Pantheist; however, Existentialism may have its positivity, yet no singular philosophy gets the goose to fart golden eggs; therefore, Oprah is lost unto her own impressive self, being blindly backward upon many a topic, yet she has an uncanny resilience that seeps forth from her almond-shaped, chocolate brown eyes. Too, she likes for many a homosexual to "come out", making stronger the fabric of a more gay America though blind to Plato's revelation about the birth of love concerning an older man and young, yummy little boy. All in all—it's bullshit, yet Oprah outshines with megabucks, mind-melding her followers into the essence of her official offspring. She is truly the first Super Villain on planet Earth.

ELISABETH HASSELBECK: Bottled blonde bombshell armed with cupcake cleavage; also, is by "straight marriage" related to the most humble Quarterback on the pro-football circuit. Anyway, Lis suffers from the same thing as Sean Hannity and Glenn Beck—she desires not freedom for America, but a theocracy crowned in the fashion of her personal morality; indeed, she has wicked ways that ensnare the uneducated, trapping blue collar men in the noose of intellectual neglect; specifically, she belly moans her internal morals, hoping for a more "controlled and docile" America.

LADY GAGA: Obviously coo-coo for Coco Puffs, and a deliberate Dago clothed in the fashion of that 1980's, scif-fi television shown dubbed "Buck Rogers" where Twiki (the rascally robot) went: "B,B,B,B,"—Moreover, supports gay rights though brilliantly blind to the negative aspects of sensationalized sodomy that leads to ulcerative colitis, H.I.V., and a plethora of other perverted-pounded problems touching the truth of fecal matter for mere, sensual exhilaration. Too, she is deaf and dumb about the ferocity of frisky females making wicked mojo with monster "strap-ons" plummeting their purity into an unnatural-receiving abyss of self-satisfaction over the decency of doing something dandylicious—missionary-styled heterosexuality. But, Miss Gaga has a great "rack", so we must forgive her.

ELTON JOHN: Would not invite him (or a vampire) into my house for dinner as within the myriad of many possibilities would be that he might attempt to pedagogue me with a jism-spawned recipe for "pigs-in-a-blanket". A talent on the piano, partner to a man, and father of a young, male child which raises Spock's eyebrow concerning the enlightenment of Plato's "Symposium"—it depicting LOVE'S birth being crafted by way of a grown man's coitus with a young boy. That being said—a Saint may he be, and it's a free country, but shit happens everywhere Bubba . . .

HILLARY CLINTON: Suffers form Nixonism, which is a phobia concerning "Being Liked" by the masses. All other information is classified at this time.

STEPHEN HAWKING: Arguably, the stupidest smart man on the planet, most likely blaming a Hebrew God's resonation into the Christ then manifestation of Catholicism for his crippled nature as he deems himself to be Galileo in some temporal time shift ornamented with altruistic possibilities.

BUBBA CLINTON: Former President of the United States; furthermore, bombed an aspirin factory and suffered a forward-fluxing economy due to Reagan tax cuts years before.

KING DAVID: Usurps even Shakespeare with his poetry being read; moreover, psychotically in love with the Semite God, and he wields Goliath's incorporeally-forged sword when in battle.

FRANCIS BACON: Shakespeare's ghost inscriber.

VIRGIN MARY: Gave 50% of her genetic material to a Messiah named Jesus; plus, remained "intact" and inviolate, wedding Joseph and accepting his children from a previous marriage as the fruit of her blessed-bosom. Too, her immaculate ovaries were touched by the Jewish God at the tender age of 14, which might make God a pedophile and should usher in the freedom of myriads of men incarcerated for statutory rape; still, she is Queen of heaven and most powerful of all Saints as she retains being the human-constructer of the benevolent Christ.

WHOOPI GOLDBERG: Smokes weed and dresses like a man.

PAN: Corporeally bizarre-crafted god, having the hindquarters of a goat; specifically, god of rustic music and companion to the beauty of nymphs.

DOCTOR: Uh—my shrink . . .

DR. PHIL: Wisdom resides within his oversized cranium; however, stupidity haunts his head as well, him being blind to the decency of drug use, finding fact with fiction as wends the weak of most substance control professionals.

DR. DREW: Possibly a Pollock without a million dollar hat as was Pope John Paul # 2; anyway, idiotic to the conceited core, unaware of the altruistic nature of narcotics, finding failure in the hearts of addicts who breathe the same addictive air as himself; moreover, blind to the brilliance of bards, scholars, mystics, and the typically crazy who have championed the priceless worth of mind-enhancing substances.

DON HENLEY: Got the platinum pipes!

MARK DAVID KING: A weak-minded fool whose best folly is fornicating with himself; specifically, committed a sensuous sin with a watermelon, and he (through the Internet) communicated with homosexuals, being at least a partial aspect of faggery. Nonetheless, a believer in the birth of bravery, being bold enough to desire an unearthly gaze upon the Holy Spirit of 1776. Too, forges the fantastic of poetry and looks marvelous in drag.

JAMES JOYCE: Sculpted the best book in the English language, depicting beyond Freud the truth of large genitalia and its fascination with married women who are only receiving average intimacy when the pipe is being laid.

BILL MAHR: Sometimes really funny, especially when stoned.

FREUD: The beard worked for him . . .

RICKY MARTIN: Corporeally-pleasing *homo-erectus* resonation; plus, looks stunning with hair gel, having a smile worth the Hollywood admission of fame.

NANCY PELOSI: Hot, in an asymmetric fashion, being breasted with boldness, and a true Democrat for the mindless masses.

ODYSSESUS: The most celebrated King of Ithaca, being a draft-dodging father, husband, lover, sailor, and warrior; also, was of small stature, but barrel-chested with an Axl Rose, bass-like voice.

GALILEO: He'll hear it a million times from the modern, evolution of Catholicism, "it" going: We're sorry dude, totally . . .

DICK CHENEY: Darth Vader's adopted brother; furthermore, likes to hunt human beings, and under the rules of the English language, a true cyborg due to mechanical implants that assist his heartbeat.

MARCUS AURELIUS: Claimed that: "The gods do exist!"; moreover, dealt with an unfaithful wife, which should give hope to all the older guys like Bruce Willis since Cougarism is on the rise with desperate dudes.

JUDAS MACCABEUS: Next to King David—the ultimate fighting machine, warding off the process of Hellenization in the Holy Land, preserving autonomy and originality for the Hebrew people.

CASANOVA: Like most men, other than those with erectile dysfunction—liked the ladies.

JOSEPH, JUDAS, JUSTUS, JAMES, ASSIA, LYDIA: Through marriage, an aspect of the Holy Family.

PRINCESS LEIA: Pondered beastality with Chewbacca; however, gave the fidelity of her rebel womb to Captain Han Solo after defrosting him.

JACK KEROUAC: Coolest guy of his era; moreover, didn't need tattoos, piercings, or long hair to have that "COOL", being bigger than life, yet humble enough to put others before him—the anthropological axiom going:

Dean M-o-r-i-a-r-t-y.

POPE JOHN PAUL # 2: Magnanimous soul blessed with immaculate

intentions; specifically, supported Reagan in defeating Communism, and

will most likely be canonized in the future.

RUSH LIMBAUGH: Gallantly promotes Conservatism from a girth-laced

frame, having a sense of humor about himself as well as all the bumbling

morons in Washington.

SEAN HANNITY: Looks like the Renaissance depictions of Satan, loving

the art of confusion and arguing; moreover, no sense of humor concerning

himself, yet willing to uncouthly stick it to the next dumb bastard.

GLENN BECK: Lacks the truth of talent, yet luck is his best virtue

achieved; also, gave up drugs and liquor in order to further squash the ripe

melons of anti-oxidant fortified narcotics.

DIONYSIUS: God of wine, like Jesus, yet not only offers the decent essence of the miraculous grape, championing also the negative aspects of wine, like: Too much is too much.

SOLOMON: Son of King David, being brilliantly blessed with the wonderful wizardry of wisdom. Too, a genuine mystic, communicating with supernatural essences, such as goes the non-ficticious lore of him bottling up all the genies.

F. SCOTT FITZGERALD: College dropout and heavy drinker, having a alcohol-spiked, pewter flask glued to his hand through large parts of his life; also, jumped out of 2 story windows and made Hemingway nervous.

THOMAS PAINE: A total and true Libertarian, being sincerely uneducated but a mystic by the Bald Eagle's account, having brought down from the ranks of heaven the Holy Spirit of 1776 and subsequently infused it into the colonial brain. The cliché goes: Without the quill of Paine, the sword of Washington would never have swung.

EZRA POUND: Responsible for the spirited success of some of the greatest writers of the 20th Century; specifically, made T.S. Eliot a poetic god. Unfortunately, when overseas, Pound dabbled in Anti-Semitism, making vulgar radio rants against the Jews; hence, he was ultimately arrested and put in a gorilla cage that was shipped to the American authorities; subsequently, Pound was imprisoned in an institute for the criminally insane, all while T.S. Eliot was receiving the Noble Prize.

BARACK OBAMA: Possibly faked the protracted release of his birth certificate; still, full of magnanimous ideals during his run against John McCain, yet has failed to become a leader on the level of Kennedy or Reagan.

GEORGE WASHINGTON: Suspiciously resembles Steven Seagal with his tall stature and intense-featured countenance; moreover, chopped down a cherry tree, championed the use of Indian Cannabis, and had many a horse shot out from under him during his days of combative anthropology.

THOMAS JEFFERSON: Damn, I still wish the 2 Dollar Bills were still in mass circulation; anyway, he was and is: Virginia's greatest lover—take that Bill Clinton . . .

ANTIOCHUS THE ILLUSTRIOUS: Attempted to Hellenize the entire globe, having met resistance from the Semite Engine fueled by the mystic mojo of Judas Maccabeus.

SIDDHARTHA AND BUDDHA: Two separate entities fused into a singular soul, or a singular soul armed with a benevolent co-inhabitant—Siddhartha receiving the cosmic nature of the Buddha after rejecting asceticism for the neutral path.

KRISHNA: A handsome, blue humanoid, possibly an avatar of Vishnu, having lived on Earth for years, doing battle with the iniquity of Nephilim-spawned giants, playing juvenile yet hilarious pranks, and like Jefferson, a lover inside the eternal essence of women.

MEL GIBSON: The original Road Warrior and genius director of "Braveheart" and "The Passion Of The Christ"; however, showed his furry Beaver, and didn't gel with the couth of many a Jew; nonetheless, a tremendous talent worth saving.

NEWT GINGRICH: I have surmised that with a frosty, white beard he may look a little like Santa Claus, and he doesn't even want to tax the rich, yet suffers from the narcissistic/internal/hypersoap-operaish stuff, believing that he could actually "beat" the super-charismatic person of Obama in a presidential election.

ROY ROGERS: The singing cowboy, and his horse named Trigger was motherf&*%$#@ smart as a Texas Whip.

SAINT PETER: Some say he greets you at the gates of heaven; anyway, the first Bishop of Rome, being the Rock on which the Christ constructed His Church—though he never boasts: Can you smell what the Rock is cook'n!!!

DANTE: Poetic genius, having been escorted by Virgil through the reeking ranks of a multi-layered hell. Dismissed the Latin language for Italian when crafting his epic "The Divine Comedy", and remains a true visionary within the theological community.

JOHN MILTON: Blind as goes the brilliance of many a bard, yet had loving offspring, them assisting him in the creation of "Paradise Lost" where we witness many a fallen angel as having celestial abilities like the Green Lantern—no shit . . .

ANNE RICE: Master of the pussafication of vampires, and likes to write soft porn; still, was responsible for the steroid shot into the ass of "Twilight", and is a genuine architect of the modern, vampire lore.

DEVIL: Once Lucifer, though some argue this; anyway, an uncanny arch-angelic essence who went head to head with the Abrahamic God's Enforcer named Saint Michael; as a result, was defeated in celestial combat and thrown beyond the Sublime Perimeter, having to create a new home in the pits of Pandemonium, and was assisted by 1/3 of the Celestial Hierarchy who followed him in his defeat; however, some mystics believe that more angelic essences aligned themselves with his nefarious ideals, following his arrogant stature into the eternal abyss of a macabre eternity. Retained his supernatural powers, poisoned and raped the creation of Mother Earth, and almost impossible to keep captive or kill as goes the proof in his escape from futurity explained by the Book of Revelation.

MARK TWAIN: Scholastic exile and river boat pilot, always ornamented in the finest of attire, having created many a literary classic, yet became conflicted with God due to the cold truth of death by a loved one.

JOE CAMEL: Doesn't exist anymore, and I'm not supposed to mention him in case the Clinton Administration may resurrect its intention to kill Big Tobacco. Verily, as were the Jedi hunted down and killed by Senator Palpatine, Joe Camel suffered the same ill-fated culmination, being executed by an adulterous President. However, the future will brag: Smoking in moderation is beneficial to your health, especially if you have Alzheimer's or Inflammatory Bowel Disease.

LOT: Wife was atomized by an atomic explosion from advanced alien species.

SAINT BARTHOLOMEW: He was flayed for his faith, being the Patron Saint of burned victims, and because of this has kinship with the Maccabean Line as some of their beloved was flayed as well.

ALBERTUS MAGNUS: Mystically aware of other life within the celestial ocean, knowing God transcends the perimeter of Mother Earth.

JESUS: Genetically-forged son of the Virgin Mary's egg, being seeded by the Will of the Hebrew God into that perfect, feminine posture. Plus, taught through parables and example, being humble to the point of addressing Himself as: The Son of Man—like many a Semite Priest such as the UFO-Viewing Ezekiel of the Old Testament. Moreover, historically listed in the writings of Josephus as a "Miracle Worker", having healed many of the shapeless back to their symmetrical forms, even resurrecting a man from the dark sleep of death, before achieving His own Resurrection through an innate power contained within His own atomic mass since He had arrived from the loins of a Supernatural Seed. Furthermore, His ultimate example of Love was that He died on the Cross for all of humanities sins, proving that it was not a Jewish or Roman-enforced execution, but of his own free will since His words in "red" state: No one takes my life, but I give it freely.

MANI: Persia's greatest artist, having claimed to be the "Helper" or "HOLY GHOST" that Christ promised would come; thus, another possible incarnation of the Hebrew God, having the wisdom and sight to know that every person has an angelic twin within the spangle of the shimmering cosmos, further proving the truth of parallel Universes; nonetheless, his groovy teachings of this and things dualistic ultimately led to his beheading; next, his headless body was stuffed with straw and hung on a city wall.

PLATO: Kinda smart maybe . . .

VIRGIL: His ghost escorted the dynamic Dante through the undergloom of it all . . .

CHAZ BONO: Totally filled with the righteous rage of bravery; specifically, has consciously made himself a luminous target due to the intrinsic fibers within; moreover, morphed himself from lady 2 dude, taking the badness of backlash upon his gallant chin. Still, his Mom is kinda/sorta a weirdo.

JIM MORRISON: An Irish-laced lover of the American Injun; specifically, a poet/rocker who plowed a plethora of poontang in his day, neverminding the grotesque fact that many of his carnal accomplishments were with women in possession of unhealthy, yeasty, and down right cheesey vaginas.

JOY BEHAR: A mercury-ornamented spirit armed with the bodaciousness of a big mouth; moreover, might be a Pinko, yet has the shimmering spangle of symmetrical stems—Pushkin would give ode . . .

JOEL OSTEEN: A quixotic, charismatic man of his own phantasm; however, is obviously genuine in his preaching that offers prosperity. Too, can bench press as much as Captain America.

CARL SAGAN: Incorrect about "US" not been visited by awe-inspiring, extra-terrestrial consciousness; alas, burned the jubilance of a girthy joint and went from mathematics to linguistics for reasons of giving the average-minded man a bit of effulgent enlightenment.

ORIGEN: Why is this bad ass dude not a Saint!?! Lore suggests he castrated himself to literally follow the words of Christ—the verse (my style) spouting: "It is better to cut part of your body off that makes you sin, rather than for your entire body to burn in hellacious futurity."

CAPTAIN AMERICA: An imagined altered human who fought the "Nazi Jealousy" during World War 2; specifically, a drug-induced muscle man, though not chastised as was the decency of Barry Bonds attempting to be the ultimate, athletic machine.

BUCK ROGERS and TWIKI: Cosmological heroes in the truest sense of the term, having as much legendary suavity as the dynamic dude dubbed "Buzz" as well as his buddy John Glenn.

INTRO:

I will not be a gay man; moreover, I will not "come out" on the resonation of Oprah Winfrey's existentially pantheistic show, and God is not ubiquitous, for the Prophet Obadiah knows: "God's Eye's are too pure to look upon the wicked." Thus, God is not everywhere!!!—He is not in the Devil's lair or in the heart of an adulterer; moreover, to Oprah—life is only what you make it to a point; people can screw you into a million, blabbering smithereens or drunk drive you into an early grave and it is not your fault. Understand: There is just not the Ultimate Truth, for there is also the Ultimate Lie; indeed, evil exists, and it is as potent a force as is the sublimity of a Good God, for even the Book of Revelation shows that after a final battle, the Adder escapes once again, or: "They stab it with their steely knives, but they still can't kill the beast!"— goes the linguistic vocalization of Don Henley. And damn't: I won't be a gay man, and Sarah Palin helps me with this, haunting my lusting libido with her librarian-like smirk behind those quasi-intellectual glasses, and I'll bet she still gets passes, especially since David Lettermen proved he had a humongous crush on her during the prime of her life, making bad taste comedy, and wends the way of my heterosexuality—please Mr. Hebrew God; I'm focused on Sarah Palin's lipstick smile, and it is a good thing, driving me bizarre yet beyond the bounce of a butt pirate, and I owe her morality a curse at William Blake's wicked yet somehow noble-minded prose concerning morals; anyway, I will not be gay, and the Good, Hebrew God has company within the empyreal spangle of a Multiverse, for all of the gods exist as well as other entities adorned with the essence that Aquinas knew lived within the Celestial

Hierarchy, and it is not always your fault when you screw up, for the Adder

does penetrate the perimeter of each man's personality, and can hex you into

the eternity of Pandemonium's funtastic flames of iniquity; therefore, invoke

the decency of existence and its magnanimous creatures, using

Existentialism to its maximum potential, and whatever you do: Don't

freaking buy a pet monkey—those motherf#@$%rs will bite. Too, they

masturbate with the most intense ferocity . . . One more thing: It's Anti-

Constitutional for the American Government to declare "war" upon its own

people—that is exactly what the Drug War is. And to all Addiction

Medicine Physicians: "Deal with it!!!" Dr. Drew and Dr. Phil hate the

freedoms founded by our Libertarian Forefathers; moreover, if a man is

classified an addict; then, don't thieve away the world from him, for sobriety

is a cruel bitched clothed in the purpose of control. If a man sculpts a

snowman and can't stop the frontal lobe euphoria he is feeling; next, give

him a beer and a menthol—let him chill and find contentment. There are a

myriad of narcotics and things alike that offer the adjective of sublime;

indeed, the Drug Czar should showcase the proper use of drugs, not steal

away the potential of their essence. And like I dared to describe before:

What if Carl Sagan didn't use marijuana to help him craft linguistic axioms concerning Astrophysics? What if Kerouac didn't suck on dextroamphetamine to spawn classics or Poe with his opiates? Should we take away these books like we stigmatize athletes for steroids? Then is Captain America a nefarious steroid user and not a royal hero? Drugs offer the essence of true evolution. They contribute to tomorrow. Yet like Dionysius, the god of wine—there is both a positive and negative. Rush Limbaugh became addicted to pain killers, but why the hell should that be my problem? I've had numerous stitches, a saliva duct stone removed, inflammatory bowel disease, burns, and a few other things that granted me a prescription to pain killers, yet I did not rob a pharmacy or try to score the shit on the street after my prescription ran out. I was chill. Liked it, but got content. Lit a cigar and made a Bloody Mary—it's cool. There is no reason drugs shouldn't have the label of "sublimity" attached to them. There will always be addicts; there will always be teenagers who are stupid, but that should not infringe upon my freedoms and liberty. Check this: Elisabeth Hasselbeck went on live television and shot down the magnanimous might of K2 (synthetic marijuana)—now let me tell you of the days of high adventure: My wife cheated on me with a teenage boy, and I was crushed, becoming an exile from my once always-attached son. I moved outta state and hid from him for four years while being sober—I was a broken mess.

Then, I heard that K2 (synthetic marijuana) was legal in the state of

Tennessee, and I tried some. One week later I was back in my son's life.

After four years of being harped on by my family, friends, and doctors, it

doing me no success in reunion—I fired up the K2, and a week later I was

infused with a masculine spirit that seduced me to once again be a father;

thus, I drove to the state of Arkansas, picked up my son, and from that day

on, he spends the summers (3 months) with me every year. It was because

the marijuana gave me the goodness of guts. I felt alive and god-like.

Furthermore, the magic of the majestic herb birthed a sense of true

heterosexuality; specifically, after ingesting marijuana I was able to dismiss

homosexual fantasies, becoming ethically transfigured and bold enough to

brave the breasts of women, intrinsically knowing: BOY, GO GET U SUM

VAGINA!!! I finally understood that nobody always wins and humility is a

decent quality; plus, I learned the fact that we're all gonna get sick and die,

but being optimistic until the end fends off the fear of bodily culmination is

the right track baby. But what if I had listened to Elisabeth Hasselbeck?

What if I never puffed away on the synthetic herb and found the gift of

courage to redeem myself? What if prescription medication and morality

guided me to do nothing and continue to hide my selfish-pride from my son?

Alas, I was fashioned fantastic! Drugs are not evil. Remember the words of

Christ: "It's not what goes into a man that makes him unclean, yet that
which comes out of his heart." I'm sorry people become addicted—I never
did. I'm sorry if your teenage daughter gets stoned and spreads her legs to
her jr. high school crush—but that's not my problem. You are responsible
for your children, and I surely don't want "It takes the Village People" to
raise my child Mrs. Clinton. Would hate to be Elton John's adopted son
since I understand Plato's "Symposium" concerning the uncouthness of
homo-erotic cupidity. Hence, it takes bravery to be free. You have to be
brave to want freedom. But Sean Hannity, Glenn Beck, Elisabeth
Hasselbeck—shit, all they want is Theocracy. They want morality to be the
ruler of America, and that is a dangerous thing, for God gave us Free Will;
thus, who is man to take it away? This is America!!! This is the Cowboy
Nation!!! This is getting into fist fights on the playground and taking that
rage to the football field, suiting up and being a man. Hemingway was no
sissy, but you as an American have the right to be sissified. And I have the
right to put whatever I want into my body. If that bothers you; then move to
another Nation that lets their juvenile understanding of a deity command
their constant suffering. I love this country. She is beautiful. She is the
greatest. She is Roosevelt giving us back our booze, Kennedy outpacing the
Russians with the space race, Reagan buying the big bombs, and Sarah Palin

32

making me want to only nail sophisticated-looking women instead of another guy. Indeed, God Bless America, and may the Holy Spirit of 1776 haunt us until perpetuity explodes into the truth of EVERYTHING and Oprah transforms into a student of that which is outside her psychotic love of herself. And I'm a prick, so there . . . And one more thing: I have been on Social Security Disability for almost a decade, suffering from a raging and sanguine case of Ulcerative Colitis, Obsessive Compulsive Disorder with Psychotic Features, and numerous other conditions including constant fungal infections on the genitalia and anus, resulting in a totally sincere, anal itch. Having been ill and laid up, I have watched a plethora of political television and monitored the tapestry of talk radio—that is why I wrote this. Every freaking day I get to hear people like Elisabeth Hasselbeck and Oprah Winfrey be idiotically vociferous concerning the human condition, and for Chrissakes—it is the reason this book has been boldly birthed, for every opinion matters, especially those chiseled by the intrepid hand of truth as goes the personal privilege of blazing bards armed with the theoretical potency of linguistic axioms . . . Now, here we go:

ONE:

Loving girls, growing

Into the pimple countenance of puberty besmirching, and

I ornament my ugly

With the gay of makeup, hoping

She doesn't scope

That nasal-planted infection of underneath the dermis, for

I would die to kiss her, yet

Adolescence erupts with tragedy, for

My genitalia is below average, and

I become the FOOL in the Deck of Tarot, teased

Beyond being straight

And believing that I could never PLEASE a female;

Thus,

Wends the wicked of brainstorming gay, only

For the purpose of having pleasurable intimacy, yet

God governs my cerebral capacity, and

I ache at the thought, knowing

My biological patriarch would descend from heaven

And kick my fag ass—

Look:

Born that way, only

Noticing the similar sex;

Next,

Maybe you get a pass from the sin of it all, but

Psychologically hornswoggled into stupidity doesn't excuse the crime, nor

Does being a brat in a frat or sorority house, wanting

To experiment for sheer elation

That does embarrass a Nation;

Still,

The Bald Eagle is the best, being

The apex of COOL;

Hence,

Freedom allows as is Free Will granted (to a potential point);

However,

The theological implications of the Divine Justice System

Enforce the trait of CHARACTER upon a soul

And hedonism is not the yummy juice

It's promised to be;

Alas,

I find Sarah Palin, praying

Away the gay, and

Goes the glee in me—

It's the icon of her eating pizza with the Donald, as well as

The Democrats and their phobia concerning her

Since she is attractive

And not the goose lathered in Clinton's bondage—

Verily,

If Hillary looked like Sarah Palin, she would've been President—and

Is it my delinquency to fantasize about Sarah Palin

In order to make my gay stay away?

If I do have carnal craving for Sarah Palin

Will I be defiling a National Treasure, or

Will the ranks of Abe Lincoln

Teleport down from heaven and kick my ass

Before a mercurial retreat in the Elysian Fields

Where with his big hat he cleans up the Greeks, especially

Plato's "Symposium" that is available in every bookstore, telling

The tale of the best love

Being that homo-eroticism between a man and little boy—

Ahh, them progressive Greeks, but

The Northern Europeans slay the shit out of Loki's tricksterism, knowing

The World Serpent rapes the ocean floor,

Like this:

Mother Nature is a bitch enslaved, weeping

Through a womb molested, birthing

The same foul fates upon her soiled land;

Specifically,

The wicked seed resonates.

And the mojo of the Annunaki or Nephilim hint at Genetic Engineering

Of humanity,

Cursing us with the dualism that maybe Mani spied upon

Before they decapitated him, stuffed

His body with the harvest of straw, and

Hung that piece of dead flesh upon the city wall

Since he proclaimed to be the incarnation of the Holy Ghost,

That sublime helper who the Christ-Man promised

Would arrive upon the topography of Terra.

Anyway,

I notice Sarah Palin's legs wrapped

In the adorning fibers of hosiery, and

Heels so high that Pushkin becomes a Russian exile, penning

Prose for the American Machine, and

I think more intently upon the Palin phenomena, glad

That it thieved me away

From the Adder's infection of non-innate gayness, meaning

The guy in the fraternity

Who gives his best buddy oral sexery

After a keg of beer

And the lure of having fun—

Well,

That guy will hate himself when consciousness

Arrives the next day, possibly

Fabricating the feature of a noose

To better loose his uncool with, and

Judas was more than the simplicity of a bad man, being

Better than Dante's doom of digestion

Within the intestinal tract of Satan, getting

Morphed into the essence of pure shit

For a poopalong/scatological eternity;

Moreover,

The climax arrives in my hand, and

I grimace at the pseudo-euphoria, knowing

The end is not the best part

Yet the action itself,

And Sarah Palin exits my mind

While I wash like a Levite Priest

Wielding the weird of the Staff of God

Before budding into the anti-oxidants

Of almonds, and

Thank you Virgin Mary within, You

Ark of the Covenant—for

Denial of humanity

Leads to the supernatural.

TWO:

Illuminated face—

Pretty boy who always got teased

And called fag—

Maybe I fit the bill

Tight in my gayness, yet

I will not yield, making

Only one homo-erotic blunder;

Next,

Asceticism birthed—

My non-sodomized hand crushed with a hammer

On file it is, and

I plead with God for forgiveness;

Then,

Decorate the androgynous facial features

By way of blue-black hair razor short but glistening, and

A diamond in my tongue, getting

One cliché piece of body art, remembering

Kerouac had the most cool, never

Needing the dufus of long hair, tattoos, or piercings shimmering

With neon glow beyond all those that rocked and rolled

Their infliction of corporeal stupidity upon themselves, and

That diamond in my tongue

To level the playing field sexually,

Wisdom allowing me the coax of Casanova, spreading

Out a labia and finger penetrating

With licks upon the masculine feature of a female

Till climax billows bright into a countenance that deserves

Since it has labored hard

With genitalia abused

For being less than average, and

Should I feel guilty to please a lass;

Moreover,

To dream of carnal contact

With the prescription

Of an almost President sculpted

By the groove of a culture conservative, and

Even the Progressives dig the hair, fixed

Up in a bun, eclipsing

The suavity of Princess Leia's design

Till stupefication is rumored, ruining

The angelic blade that is Sarah Palin's bewitching beauty,

A blade forged by angels to slay angels, having

A cognizance locked within

It's holy steel.

I make sense, and

The electric news on Fox gives me humble girth—

Better to fantasize adultery

With a potent women

Than get oversexed with parts that match, making

The truth of FAG.

Look, it's a nasty word, yet

For those not spawned with the intrinsic desire

To heavy pet their own gender—

It is an abomination of gluttony, satisfying

Till guilt rips

With the reason of lovemaking being something natural

And divine, constructed

For the purpose of giving!

I have no guilt when I dream about Sarah Palin, yet

I know the theological axiom of Christ-Man concerned, offering

The words that if it is even in your heart you are a sinner, and

Better for me to be a bit of a rebel

Than to wrestle

With my own gender till crippling climax, scorning

My loins till I shout out a Davidian Psalm, knowing

He was the best King

And bard,

Circumcised with wisdom in his seed

That still blessed the birth of Solomon, genetically, yet

King David was the best of men—

God's favorite! Truly, for

No other loved the Hebrew conception of the Supernatural Patriarch

More than a brave boy

Who did smite Goliath with a sling

For the simple reason that he bad-mouthed the Semite's main Deity;

Next,

Taking the hybrid giant's blade—

It too forged by angels to kill angels, slicing

Off the behemoth head, storing

The use of the sharp weapon

In an armory for the further purpose of war.

But loving God drives man to more than killing, for

The young King that is David does weep

With the humiliation

Of sexually-transmitted diseases, even

Though cautious enough

To dismiss coitus with concubines gone slut mode, for

The honor in his pelvic region

Outshined the innate, anthropological hell of our molested creation—

God not able to rid the Garden

Of an Adder's entrance into our DNA, and

All is lost

Lest you love the Father,

Obedient,

Even unto the state of death, where

Corporeal cessation offers illuminative knowledge

Till genetics clone, and

Consciousness is trapped even in a single cell, offering

The truth of resurrection, and

Reincarnation seems a melodious maxim as well,

It being hinted upon by the futurity of humanity

Knowing how to an avatar make, and

In the next days of man

Will the GENETIC REVOLUTION

Ignite us to the state of gods

That King David did Psalm,

Wise enough, even

More than any Republican

Who crushes the nature of science

That needs the co-action of religion, and

Once united,

All the mojo of things supermundane appear

With accepted brilliance, for

The days down the road of humanity

Are best served not with caution, yet

The intrepid guile

Of a God courageous enough

To birth children that may hate Him, and

Superman LIVES! Tomorrow indeed

He arrives,

Not with a cape and blue pajamas, yet

Adorned in the axiomatic glow

Of science gelled with religion, accepting

The stupidity of Stephen Hawking

As well as the Protestant ignorance of mindless Creation;

Specifically,

With mathematics we can't read the mind of God, for

We can't even read the mind of an ant;

Thus,

Stephen Hawking loathes theological wisdom, and

Myriads of Christians discount the duty of science;

Hence,

The Adder enjoys the lack of matrimony,

Him knowing that he will only be found

And defeated

Once the TWO merge in mystical alliance, offering

Up the eternal life of humanity, existing

Till the Angelic Wars

Tame the torrid trauma

Fed to us by the adder.

But now:

We are dieing—

Food for the Earth.

* * * * * *

Heinz Field, Pittsburgh; specifically, it is a stroke near the madness of midnight, the full moon aglow like an effulgent piece of neon-green cheese; plus, the celestial ocean of stars spangle the black canvass of the Megaverse, and below, illuminated by the creation of Adam's invention, the quasi-turf billows bright, allowing the talkative players on the field to scope each other out; however, no one resides as an audience—only the debaters are deemed destine for their symposium upon the American condition. So, the scene goes: Four potent women reclining erectly at a circular table with whiskey, coffee, wine, and a grape soda fixed in their rightful and respected hands—them drinking as the night digests the day.

SARAH PALIN

Like drop the "F" bomb on me all you want; I'm certified—a real, gosh darn celebrity.

OPRAH WINFREY

Celebrity is only a status achieved upon visitation of my show.

VIRGIN MARY

Remember the words of Mark David King in his *Internal Gospel,* for it says:

God has His own celebrities.

OPRAH WINFREY

I just can't agree with that.

WHOOPI GOLDBERG

Does anybody have a joint?

SARAH PALIN

Nobody is paying attention girl.

OPRAH WINFREY

I am special; I have ignited not only the Obama Presidency, and believe

me—it had nothing to do with me being a card-carrying African-American;

plus, Ricky Martin "came out" on my show.

SARAH PALIN

Like wake up and smell the Folgers Oprah. You gotta pray away the gay.

Instead of "coming out" you gotta "come home" to the truth of a

sophisticated nature.

VIRGIN MARY

Sarah sports sublimity in attempting to tame the torrid desires of a world

wending wickedways. The practice of asceticism births the best in the

human machine. Look at me—I inherited perpetual virginity and forged the

Messiah within my wondrous womb when I was only 14 years of age, and I didn't act like a snotty Republican by trying to get God arrested for rape. Furthermore, Martin Luther bailed on asceticism and he constructed Protestantism out of his own inability to hack it, further putting a theological choke hold on my decency, and even He (JESUS) knows: You can say stuff about me, but don't you dare criticize My mother. Too, Siddhartha bailed on asceticism and inherited the Buddha, yet if he would've been determined with being an ascetic, he may have inherited an even more potent, super entity such as That which Is Jehovah.

OPRAH WINFREY

You are not still a Virgin; the Protestants . . .

SARAH PALIN

Don't you dare pry inside her benevolent womb, that Tower of Ivory, inviolate, undefiled piece of God's romantic heart. She is like a wife, a Queen to the King of the Megaverse, and canonized text is ambiguous, but many uncanonized pieces of material, including the Gnostic writings prove her to have married Joseph when he was already blessed with offspring— them being: Judas, Justus, James, Assia, Lydia.

WHOOPI GOLDBERG

What about a bong hit? Holla if ya hear me.

OPRAH WINFREY

Thank God the 60's saved America. Free Love, Civil Rights, and the culmination of the Dirty Draft.

SARAH PALIN

The 60's? What the "F"? Listen, back in the 50's we had it made—yeah, back then before the bitches burned the bra. Listen sister—Free Love is skank love. In the 50's you found your sweetheart in high school or college; next, you married and meshed for eternity, but after the 60's you don't stay loyal to your adolescent sweetheart; instead, you pimp yourself out to the possibilities of carnal stupidity, and every teenager in this country will have a broken heart at one time or another, for Free Love has robbed them of the possibility of fidelity, though may it resonate in the minds and hearts of all good folk fuelled with blood flow and ovarian loyalty.

WHOOPI GOLDBERG

Ya, ovarian loyalty. Ladies, uh—I'm sorry, I think I just burned a blunt before I came out here. So whatta 'bout a menthol. Ya'll got a KOOL for a sister?

OPRAH WINFREY

I have seen God.

VIRGIN MARY

I basically married Him.

SARAH PALIN

The Virgin wins. But shit, have you guys ever shot a moose—Hemingway

had stones.

OPRAH WINFREY

When you Republicans shoot things you never get in trouble, not even if its

Dick Cheney, but God forbid a Liberal have an affair . . .

WHOOPI GOLDBERG

I hear ya. I hear ya.

THREE:

Lady Gaga doesn't know crap;

However,

She has a great rack.

And the mere rhymester that is rap, giving

James Joyce further a complex

Considering a wife's affair, and

The best novel sculpted, him

Being the mightiest bard in the English language

Save Shakespeare himself, yet

We all know it was really Francis Bacon, and

Nobody cares anymore

But mystery galore is Sarah Palin's panty drawer;

Alas,

The face,

Those glasses,

Legs wrapped

In the electric fashion of black stockings and heels

Resurrecting better than Viagra

And Fitzgerald's Roaring 20's defined

By her being the sexy school teacher,

The private tutor,

The librarian like I scribed before;

Moreover,

Not even the heat-seeking missile

Of Bubba Clinton

Had more shock and awe

In an anthropological sense

Than the outline of Palin's aura, shining

Platinum,

Between silk sheets—

And why the hell does Newt Gingrich think he can beat Obama?

Has anyone

Dreamed the illusion of Gingrich

Crowned atop

The thunderous gallop

Of a steed, like

That one Roy Rogers trained

To do basic mathematics, using

A hoof instead of a slide rule?

And the military, inside

That killing machine

The Progressives taint

With social experiments, and

Let's go to battle boys, but

First we must witness the foulness

Of an erection in communal showers;

Then,

Go kill the enemy after seeing that big one, for

The best hunters are Freudian's freaked

By the fear of their own homosexuality;

Alas,

Palin again—Miss Sarah, strutting

Like a luscious lass

Beating me with the Nun of a ruler

Between the shoulder blades—

And I like it!

Give me more, for

The daymare of being under the sheets with another man

In harmonious motion

And sweet chatter

Makes the molester's choad

Elongate fatter and wide

Till self-hatred, and:

"I'm sorry Dad! I'm sorry! You played college football, and I'm a fag."

It is true.

Test the wombs of women creaming the junk

Of a sororities brainwash

Into the culture of Greek—

Antiochus the Illustrious fixated

Upon the process of Hellenization, and

The Jews revolt with magical rebellion, giving

A kick in the ass

With a superior theology

Till the Maccabeus line

Put in the frying pan births

Saint Bartholomew to be their Patron Saint, and

Hanukkah does ignite

The glory of a God and people

Who will NOT DIE!

Don't screw with the JEWS!

They don't have ninjas, samurais, or Navy Seals, but

Those members of the Tribe

Are upon the physical branch of a Superior God, spawned

For the purpose of His pleasure, extending

A way in for all of us

Through the unearthly extension of the olive branch by the Christ—this

Is the mojo

Of magnanimous mystics

Hellbent

Upon the purpose

Of decency.

Moreover,

Bill Maher is not Thomas Paine

In the least, defaming

Not sincerely as much

Or secretly penning Washington's Journals

Or the love machine of downtown

Like Jefferson bedding the blacks, and

A racist will say:

"It's every black man's dream to have a white woman."

Yet Jefferson

Was intrepid

Before the dawn

Of the days of DISCO

Digging deepwards

With dingalings descending

For the sensation of sheer elation

As goes the weakness

Of the human machine

Unevolved

And non-cyborgish

Till a futurity

Allows perfection

By way of cerebral control

Through our own autonomy

Saved by the wave of Old Glory—

No one wants a Good bitch to die!!!

FOUR:

She is scarlet, an

Emerald angel hued spectacular—

Look,

It's true,

Sarah Palin is babalicious non-stick bubble gum

Chewed pink till enlightenment, and

Who cares if she lacks the intellectual fabric

Of Obama's Intelligent Quotient, for

She is divine with fidelity, embracing

The union of matrimony

Till eternity allows diversity

Within the winding wheels of change, spinning

With perpetuity, and

I dream of taking her glasses off

And letting down that majestic mane

Pinned up like a cute Betty

Till I glare into those chocolate browns, and

It is better than male intercourse

Into me, birthing

Not the natural nature of a baby, but

Ulcerative Colitis out of remission, and

Why the hell is Elton John celebrated

For gay union with a male child—

You think that kid will have the hope of heterosexuality

If not maligned

By the suspicious eyes of Plato reminding

Why tragedy is best admitted by the Greeks, and

Elton John thieves with mercury

The innocence of a soul golden, giving

The haunt of sexual asymmetry

To a consciousness developed by the evolution of a Hebrew God—

And they say:

Smite the Semitic Engine

That doth produce morality and character, for

She is a cruel bitch

Clothed in Pound's botched humanity, yet

Nothing does eclipse the reverence of the Christ-Man, instructing:

"Salvation comes from the Jews."

Take that Mel Gibson

On fire with the blood of Romans

Deep and sanguine into his fingers, fiddling

With angels fallen

For contempt of a culture

That will not die

But resonate until the birth of the GENETIC REVOLUTION

And beyond.

Uh-hum . . .

I think about Sarah Palin when I go gay

And it dissolves into an adulterous sin

Yet saves from the diabolical action

That ashed Lot's wife into a pillar of salt

By way of an alien's nuclear explosion

As mystically scribed by a Biblical bard . . .

* * * * * *

I'm on the sophisticated telepathy of my shrink's couch—him a Harvard

man and Freudian, to the jaw bone. I am clothed in conservative attire,

sucking down a menthol and spilling the bodacious beans of my life to the

Doctor.

MARK

I've had gay thoughts; moreover, I've contacted gay guys on the Internet;

then, I fall asleep and wake up stupefied. Totally, I erase all my Internet

desires, and I beg the God of Israel to strike me down. I don't wanna be a

fag. I don't wanna disrespect my biological father who resides in the grave.

But I feel that I can't please a woman. Verily, I have only had sexual

intercourse with one woman my entire life, and she told me that I was a terrible man in the sack; indeed, the vultures circle every bed of a woman I may desire to be intimate with; thus, I have gone gay, having once even touched a man but no sodomy; next, I pulverized that hand with a hammer, went to the Emergency and got it put in a splint with a prescription for pain pills; still, I believe myself evil for gay thoughts, and I beg the angels and saints to transfigure me. To evolve me into a bio-mechanical essence whereas I can program my libido to be docile and undetermined. That is my folly and desire.

DOCTOR

Are you still taking your medication—those anti-psychotics and all the rest.

MARK

Yes, but I still feel like a macabre soul infected with diabolical demons driving me to dastardly deeds. My only escape into contentment is the nirvana of Sarah Palin naked within the theater of my mind, clothed in pump-me heels and echoing a Sirenian song to my character of Odysseus.

DOCTOR

You're sick Mark. But you gotta deal . . .

MARK

If only you could remove a testicle or something; then I'd feel much better.

FIVE:

Kablaam!!!

And the worst of all:

INSIDE EDITION

Spilling

Facial distortion—

A chimp tears off the face too on Oprah

And the pics desired

By those lacking in mercy.

Worst things:

Facial mutilation;

Plus,

Genitalic mutilation;

Then

Wends the weird of a scrotum detached

And castrated a zillion times over

Is the superfluidity of Christ crucified, being

The best of humanity

Torn away from appreciation of sex, and

Even Krishna beds the babes, yet

The ichor of the Christ runs pure, being

The flow of a Semitic Motor (most likely a V-8)

Past the Chi

In Siddhartha;

Indeed,

Why do the Protestants hate the Virgin Queen?

Her splendor being the simplicity

Of utter decency.

Better than the platinum Dove

Of His own Trinity

Did the Father see hope

In the ovaries of a 14 year old mystic, communicating

With the fabric of fine feathers

Angel spawned;

Alas,

Jesus might be more than merely

A 50% genetic duplicate, yet

The seed offers the sex of the child

And the Holy Queen's egg

Is the acquiesce of life

Into her

Forever, giving

Might to the fight

Against the adder

And his minotaur-like minions

Devouring the Milky Way

And beyond—

Saint Albertus Magnus knowing of other life

Within the cosmological conclusion

Of it all

As did a Franciscan-frying Milton

Burnt with visions

Yet dumb to the defense of Catholicism

Haunting with asceticism

As goes the deepest commitment

And most chiseled mind

Of a mystic warrior

Subservient

To the Truth of a Hebrew God

And not the pussafication

Of theology crafted by the wickedness

Of Anne Rice

Or the Twilight Saga

Lacking the love of punishment

Into it's own self, mutilating

God's best grace upon our own selves;

Hence,

My face is ripped apart

But not by a chimpanzee, and

I was celibate for over a decade

In the depths of adulthood

As coitus

Was interrupted

By the phobia of myself

Missing the value of self-confidence

Blown into my nostrils

By a biological Dad pre-destined to die

Before my age as a man;

Thus again

Goes my daydreaming loins

Into lusting for Sarah Palin

As anything is better than gay

For me.

But you boy.

You raised by Elton John

And a fag deemed by Daddy

Are the real deal

And Saint Peter pushes past the Sublime perimeter, but

I can't sell snow cones in hell

For extra capitalism

As wends the way

Of fear pushing me past heterosexuality

Cause I'm chicken shit

To put my package

Into the receiving box of a fabulous female

Who methinks

Transcends my carnal trickery

Into convincing her corporealness

To starburst with climax, meaning:

If orgasm is scored

Am I okay?

Or is it the length and width of it all, making

Me slap Marcus Aurelius

And fantasize myself as another man

Born with the colossal dong

Banging the best of women.

Alas,

Sarah Palin again, and

For a retarded reason

Since I am a puny man

Hating my own orgasm

As I only want to please my dreamgirl, yet

Real-Life proves me lacking, and

I see the severity of Internet Porn, knowing

That I can't "complete" the vagina;

Thus,

I fairy fagwards, festering

With the fury

Of salacious stupidity

Barking out the ecstasy

Of being filled to the max, and

That is my nefarious nature

Unless

Sarah Palin strips me of perfection, allowing

The humility of regularity or less, and

What of them painted with no faces,

Lost to an accident

Without the interference

Of God's protection, and

They curse the Almighty

As did Twain,

Not knowing

The devil desires dependence

Upon the destruction

Of his own devious daymare

Into the hearts and truths of human people.

SIX:

I will not pester Joe Camel

In a court of law;

Specifically,

Freudian jaw cancer sleeps

In my corporeal form, yet

I rolled the dice

As do we all

In the art of being human.

My Grandma lived to be 87 years old

Eating 2 packs a day—

The breakfast of champions, and

Hers were 100's;

Hence,

Beyond the ordinary of 2 packs a day

And cancer did avoid her.

There are worse things than death;

Plus,

The Grim Reaper

Is a talented bluffer, and

Heaven can seem a mirage

Yet hell has been tested by the best of men, and

If you die and wake up encompassed by a legion of fallen angels;

Then

Kick the shit outta them

And dare an escape, for

Hell cannot hold the best of intentions, and

Neither can heaven pulse with somber spirits;

Thus,

Be alive in the passion of God, knowing

Positivity constructed the world

And negativity is the flu symptoms tearing it down, making

Men weak with fits of rage, and

They fight like hoodlums

On the street, yet

The real man saves it for the field of play, spearing

The adversary when it is legal, and

Nothing trumps contact sports

For the good of man's libido, allowing

Him to know what toughness is

Rather than finding himself intoxicated

And stupid

Within the confines of a bar

And fisticuffing for the attention of a fast girl.

Being a man means: Accepting Death.

Futurity promises resurrection and reincarnation—

The GENETIC REVOLUTION birthing the proof of 2 varying theologies

Axiomatically happening and freak'n

The minds of atheists

Haunted by their own vacuous spirits—

But of now:

Return to death, for

That is the only way to travel further

Into a state of possibilities.

Don't be cremated

Or leave no trace of resonating DNA, for

Who will clone consciousness remembered

When the Democratic Party

Resurrects all the wraiths in cemeteries

500 years from now?—

Tongue in check, but truly, and

I can feel the tumor, yet

I will not lay in bed and allow death to overcome me, but

I will leap and jump into oblivion, and

If I see a lake of fire;

Next,

I will do a cannon ball into my infamy

For the enjoyment

Of all souls and essences

Laughing in Empyrean

As did the gods

Upon the glimmering glance of symmetrical Pan.

* * * * * *

We are all, nothing, but a bunch of sons of bitches . . .

. . . fini . . .

AFTERTHOUGHT:

I would have been good at being gay; however, resistance towards temptation is the fuel in the Semitic Engine of the Almighty God, as I have beforehand mentioned. Regardless, we all have to follow our own paths, and this being a "supposed" Free Country we have the right to wend wickedways if we want, or stroll through the effulgent spangle of supersublimity. No man is Superman. Not yet anyway. But the GENETIC REVOLUTION will make us all what Nietzsche fathomed in his psychotic brainstorm. If a solar flare doesn't damn the Earth, or if advanced weaponry doesn't diminish us to dust; then indeed, we will have achieved eternal humanity, and most likely be included into the cosmological community. Until then, we have the plight of being backward, uneducated, and voodooed by our lack of imagination and dismissal of morally-existing Deities. There is not only God, but bad motherf%&*@#$s as well, and for now: We are all vehicles sculpted by the passengers who wish to manipulate us, and this way or that way do they steer us, all according to their own immortal lusts. Totally—Good Luck . . .

- fini –

Somebody stop me—I'm tell'n ya; nevertheless, it gets worse, totally dude. Check this:

The Pits of Pandemonium are not lewdly laced in fire, for

73

Hell is a playground, encompassing

The wicked—

It is the goddamn glory

Of being a cheat, fink, rapist, or murderer without sublime bull's eye;

Indeed,

Like Vegas Baby—24/7 does Hell blast the Rock'n Roll, getting

High for mundane purpose, and

Laboring in the art of humanities further deception, knowing

Most come here, where

The Devil is—

Throned upon the fun squish of a breast-implanted beanbag, wielding

The weird of a penis-like scepter, and

Eternally igniting things dubious

To damn the decency of a Hebrew God

And all the altruistic lesser gods who reside beneath;

Alas,

Weep not for the sinner armed with the clarity of confidence, for

His is a splendid stay

In the mire of the minotaur, and

The mentally handicapped killer is lost unto Limbo, stagnating

Further without the ghosty/cerebral capacity

To attain the attention of Heaven, Her

Billowing bright yet dead with the popular people, housing

Only the infamy of losers gone sublime, torturing

Themselves and measuring their own feces

As goes the cruel truth

Of the good guy finishing last.

Verily,

Who would want to inherit Heaven?

They don't have orgies there

Or the crack pipe to smoke;

Moreover,

Hell is the place to party, and

Even after the sulfur-burning lake lasts maybe a millennia—

Resurrection belongs to the Beast and his myriads of minions

Loving the fact

That God lets His own people

Reside in the squalor

Of resistance.

Yep,

Heaven is a junkyard—

There is no bling bling there, for

The Devil did penetrate the Bible, and all Holy Texts, crafting

The lies contained within, at least a partial portion—

Enough to make Joel Osteen say:

Luv ya sum Jesus, and the greenbacks grow!

Was Solomon's fate not fickle

Though frugal he was not, and

Christ, bizarre as a hobo, lover of chastity, lover of poverty, and

Strength of confessors

Offers not Internet porn in heaven, and

What female spirit reborn

Would wish to hang with the everlast

Of a eunuch made

As the ascetic Origen, adorned in perfect passion

Cuts loose on his own scrotum

To Christ please.

If you die and wanna fuck—

Be a crazy ass, suicide-bombing Muslim or Capitalistic Protestant

Who thinks Heaven's road will be paved in platinum.

Again: Hell is a playground, and

All the cool souls get to go there, finding

Contentment in over-doing things, like

Jim Morrison merging the mojo of LSD and shrooms

To better bang a bitch, but

That herb is holy, not

To be perverted by the quicksand of fame

Vortexing with vacuous intentions

The tits

Of all Hollywood stars

Into the belly of the beast.

Come on—

Who would wanna hang with a Virgin Queen, or

A plethora of ascetics, perpetually resisting, or

A celibate demi-God who dumped on the Devil;

Indeed,

The Devil asked Jesus:

"Hey son of man—want some pussy? Riches? Power?"

To which Christ denied Himself

The demonic digestion of it all, constructing

A kingdom where salvation

Is seen for what it truly is—a home for the loser.

The poor SOB who denied himself his own life—

That is the magic of a man on his way to Heaven, and

Now I hear the population hate me all the more—

It gelled with the grotesque grunts of demons

Damning my mind, monitoring

Me—infusing me further with delicious desire to reveal my ass, and

Buster: It's better to bust your own ass

Than to achieve hedonistic epiphany, for

God's intention is not our gregarious glee, yet

A sacrifice of oneself

In the everlasting flux of things fantastic, only

Taking what you truly need

And distributing the rest of the purse

To the propaganda of blessed shallowness—

Tough Love can BITE ME, for

Compassion cures a man, allowing

The grace of a path shown

To flower into the fruits of Eden squashed, but

Refurnished by the humble, loving

God more than themselves, and

Trying to understand through rigorous contemplation

The necessity of loving that which is ugly, for

Eternity in God's Kingdom

Is way cool plastic surgery, and brother—

I need me sum . . .

Uh, I hate to do this, but I will:

The State of Tennessee haunts the hopes of the diseased

With cruel intentions;

Indeed,

You can have legal Crystal Meth in Tennessee, yet

Not the anti-inflammatory and anti-oxidant known as Marijuana.

Just a glimpse into the gimp that I am—

CURRENT MEDICATIONS:

FLUOXETINE, 80 mg—take once daily, a Selective Serotonin Reuptake Inhibitor, having side effects that cause loose stools, hair loss, and the inability to sexually orgasm, just to name a few.

RISPERIDONE, 1 mg—take up to 3 daily, being an anti-psychotic, having the side effects of hair loss, dizziness, production of mammary glands on males; plus, there is the gayish/girlishness of possible lactation for males.

ZYPREXA, 20 mg—take once daily, which sedates the brain and causes deep, coma-like sleep.

VYVANSE, 70 mg—legal Crystal Meth basically, having the side effects of possible heart problems, agitation, and uncontrollable shaking to name some.

ASACOL—gives symmetry to an inflamed and ulcerated colon

REMICADE INFUSION—used when necessary, which puts ulcerative colitis into a state of remission, yet possibly makes you prone to infections, especially fungal; plus, tuberculosis is a tangible threat to the body being treated.

PREDNISONE—when needed, and it can break down your bone mass; moreover, causes obesity and the maddening severity of adult acne—more like plague-inspired boils in my face's case.

APEXICON E CREAM: Fights Psoriasis, yet not if it is raging.

KETOCONAZLE CREAM: Fights the mushrooms in the damp part of my rectum.

But Know: This medication has actually helped me, allowing for a semi-normal life among the glistening masses of the non-zombie! Truly, all of my physicians were noble in their pursuit of my treatment, and without the arsenal of medication, as I experienced it in my 20's, life was not worth living, and I spent a splendid amount of time torturing myself further into the intrepidness of insanity during those younger years.

MY ILLNESSES:

Ulcerative Colitis—at times, up to ten mind-numbing bowel movements daily; also, very bloody at times, causing me to become anemic and at one point need a blood transfusion. Fumbling fecal accidents in my trousers are common, forcing me to carry cleaning utensils if going somewhere social, and nervousness produces the swift exodus of bowels as well—there is no stopping the mercurial flux of diarrhea either, whether bloody or dark black, it exploding from my rectum at least a few times on a monthly basis; plus, toxic smelling gas erupts from my ass neck numerous times daily, and I am prone to oddly lay on the ground naked and pull forth the grossness of poop from between my butt cheeks as constipation is a bi-monthly antagonization.

Anal Fungus: Most likely, a side effect of the numerous REMICADE Infusions, requiring anti-fungal to knock out the mushrooms growing in my ass. Verily, it is a sincere, anal itch, ushering in depression, ass pain and blood when scratched; furthermore, makes it impossible to sit down without one of those doughnut things.

Psoriasis: Over anal area; plus, in ears and on penis, being painful and sanguinely smeared if itched or rubbed, making it damn near difficult to wipe buttocks clean or casually masturbate—I've been celibate now for 5 years, and this did not cause me to be a homo-searching pedophile, so neither will celibacy have that effect on a heterosexual, Catholic priest.

Obsessive Compulsive Disorder with Psychotic Features: Visions of spiders, goblins, angels (aliens), and demons that are vociferously obnoxious in my head, forcing me into many a mystical ritual to cleanse the spiritual contagion; however, sometimes the angelic chatter is pleasant though monstrously mysterious; also, inability to think straight due to a complex of always being germ free and sin free. Masturbation and sexual fantasies produce mortification of the senses, asceticism, and a Levite-Like washing of the body, especially pubes. Subsequently starved myself to 117 pounds due to obsession driving me to compulsively ponder if I had oral cancer, which made me constantly check the insides of my mouth, this rudely resulting in crippling cracks at the corners of my oral cavity that will not heal, even after years of medication, making it impossible for me to have dental procedures or to take a big bite of food; moreover, made me become a vegetarian, knowing Krishna had a pet cow and revealed himself to me walking on radiant beams of the effulgent Sun; furthermore, to cure my fiction-like, oral cancer, I crazily gobbled up the goodness of numerous, raw garlic cloves daily, and I lavishly devoured uncanny amounts of lycopene-fortified tomato paste for years, washing it down with unearthly amounts of green tea and aloe juice; as a result, I developed Ulcerative Colitis, having burned a gapping hole in my large intestine. Too, I boldly beat myself repeatedly, which required cat scans, and I locked myself in closets for punishment due to sexual fantasies as well as loaded my back down with opprobrium and mimicked the march to Calvary for hours on end; also, lacerated self for 2 decades, face mostly—one such time with a broken coke bottle that required 12 stitches below the cheekbone as I was, in the art of synergy, trying to remove a cyst that made me more corporeally unpleasing and rightfully inflicting justice upon my own lousy soul. Too, sleep paralysis (possible from medication), creating the inability to scream for help as I sometimes become numbly locked in the theater of my mutated mind and groveled over by fallen, angelic aliens.

Epididymitis: Scrotum grows to large size, becoming inflamed—most likely due to microscopic, funky nastiness strategically crawling inside the holiness of my blessed urethra.

MY QUESTION:

Why can't I get Medical Marijuana in my state!?????????????????!

I can have legal Meth-Like substance to keep me awake due to lethargy from

high doses of brain sedating, anti-psychotics. So, whatz the problem Chief?

Marijuana reduces inflammation and is an anti-oxidant; it can be absorbed in

fat and eaten if being smoked seems salacious to the reluctant respiratory

system; however, may actually protect lungs from the carnivore of cancerous

happenings. Too, offers cerebral control in many users, eclipsing psychotic

thoughts (even the supposed happenings of toxic psychosis) with the

potency of confidence and belief in oneself (in my case), making for a

contributing member of non-delinquent society. And I don't care if pieces

of adolescent crap abuse it for sex parties—I want this medicine, and would

be able to reduce my pill intake by half; plus, all of my homosexual thoughts

ceased to exist during the use of marijuana, it taking me to the sublimity of

straightness—what's more Republican than that? And you Democrats too—

start giving a damn about the deafening disaster of the Drug War, for isn't it

Anti-Constitutional for the American Government to declare War upon its

own people? And that is exactly what the Drug War is. Shit, I'm pooped

after being this crazy ass scribe. Get in line State of Tennessee!!! The Bible

Belt is giving me a hernia, and I'll bet I love Christ's Passion more than you

. . .

. . . totally, fini . . .